Kakeibo

Art of saving money

Budget Book

Annual Revenues and Expenses

Month	Income	Expenses

Notes

....
....
....

Annual savings targets

$

Month

Month by month note the savings

$

$

$

$

$

$

$

$

$

$

$

$

Month :

Family Account

Beginning of month

.... $

Savings Account

Beginning of month

.... $

Income

Date	Description	Amount
		$
		$
		$
		$
		$

Total $

Fixed Expenses

Date	Description	Amount
		$
		$
		$
		$
		$
		$
		$
		$
		$
		$
		$
		$

Total $

How much i want to save : .... $

Income   Fixes Expenses   Savings Goal

.... $ —   .... $ —   .... $

=

Money available

$

Estimated spending money

	Week 1	Week 2	Week 3	Week 4	Week 5
Date					
Estimated spending money					
Expenses					

Notes

. . . .

. . . .

. . . .

My categories

1 ....
2 ....
3 ....
4 ....

Date	Category	Description	Amount
			$
			$
			$
			$
			$
			$
			$
			$
			$
			$
			$
			$
			$
			$
			$
			$
			$
			$
			$
			$
			$
			$
			$
			$
			$
			$
			$
			$
			$
			$
			$

Total | $

Total expenses

Categories

1 .... $

2 .... $

3 .... $

4 .... $

Fixes expenses   .... $

Total expenses   [$]

Total income   .... $

Total expenses   .... $

Money saved   .... $

Spending wheel

Improvement action

. . . .

. . . .

. . . .

. . . .

Notes

. . . .

. . . .

. . . .

. . . .

Month :

Family Account

Beginning of month

.... $

Savings Account

Beginning of month

.... $

Income

Date	Description	Amount
		$
		$
		$
		$
		$

Total $

Fixed Expenses

Date	Description	Amount
		$
		$
		$
		$
		$
		$
		$
		$
		$
		$
		$
		$

Total $

. . . .
. . . .

How much i want to save :   . . . . $

Income		Fixes Expenses		Savings Goal
. . . . $	—	. . . . $	—	. . . . $

=

Money available

$

Estimated spending money

	Week 1	Week 2	Week 3	Week 4	Week 5
Date					
Estimated spending money					
Expenses					

Notes

. . . .
. . . .
. . . .

My categories

1 . . . .

2 . . . .

3 . . . .

4 . . . .

Expenses

Date	Category	Description	Amount
			$
			$
			$
			$
			$
			$
			$
			$
			$
			$
			$
			$
			$
			$
			$
			$
			$
			$
			$
			$
			$
			$
			$
			$
			$
			$
			$
			$
			$
			$
			$

Total $

Total expenses

Categories   1 . . . . $

                    2 . . . . $

                    3 . . . . $

                    4 . . . . $

Fixes expenses   . . . . $

Total expenses   [$]

Total income   . . . . $

Total expenses   . . . . $

Money saved   . . . . $

Spending wheel

Improvement action

. . . .

. . . .

. . . .

. . . .

Notes

. . . .

. . . .

. . . .

. . . .

Month :

Family Account

Beginning of month

.... $

Savings Account

Beginning of month

.... $

Income

Date	Description	Amount
		$
		$
		$
		$
		$

Total $

Fixed Expenses

Date	Description	Amount
		$
		$
		$
		$
		$
		$
		$
		$
		$
		$
		$
		$

Total $

. . . .

. . . .

How much i want to save : . . . . $

Income		Fixes Expenses		Savings Goal
. . . . $	−	. . . . $	−	. . . . $

=

Money available

$

— ⋇ — Estimated spending money — ⋇ —

	Week 1	Week 2	Week 3	Week 4	Week 5
Date					
Estimated spending money					
Expenses					

— ⋇ — Notes — ⋇ —

. . . .

. . . .

. . . .

My categories

1 . . . .
2 . . . .
3 . . . .
4 . . . .

Expenses

Date	Category	Description	Amount
			$
			$
			$
			$
			$
			$
			$
			$
			$
			$
			$
			$
			$
			$
			$
			$
			$
			$
			$
			$
			$
			$
			$
			$
			$
			$
			$
			$
			$
			$
			$
			$

Total $

Total expenses

Categories

1 .... $

2 .... $

3 .... $

4 .... $

Fixes expenses   .... $

Total expenses   [$]

Total income   .... $

Total expenses   .... $

Money saved   .... $

Spending wheel

Improvement action

....

....

....

....

Notes

....

....

....

....

Month :

Family Account

Beginning of month

.... $

Savings Account

Beginning of month

.... $

Income

Date	Description	Amount
		$
		$
		$
		$
		$

Total $

Fixed Expenses

Date	Description	Amount
		$
		$
		$
		$
		$
		$
		$
		$
		$
		$
		$
		$

Total $

How much i want to save : [. . . . . . . $]

Income		Fixes Expenses		Savings Goal
. . . . $	−	. . . . $	−	. . . . $

=

Money available

[$]

—— Estimated spending money ——

	Week 1	Week 2	Week 3	Week 4	Week 5
Date					
Estimated spending money					
Expenses					

—— Notes ——

. . . .
. . . .
. . . .

My categories

1. . . . .
2. . . . .
3. . . . .
4. . . . .

Expenses

Date	Category	Description	Amount
			$
			$
			$
			$
			$
			$
			$
			$
			$
			$
			$
			$
			$
			$
			$
			$
			$
			$
			$
			$
			$
			$
			$
			$
			$
			$
			$
			$
			$
			$
			$
			$
			$

 Total $

Total expenses

Categories   1 .... $

2 .... $

3 .... $

4 .... $

Fixes expenses   .... $

Total expenses   [$]

Total income   .... $

Total expenses   .... $

Money saved   .... $

Spending wheel

Improvement action

. . . .
. . . .
. . . .
. . . .

Notes

. . . .
. . . .
. . . .
. . . .

Month :

Family Account

Beginning of month

.... $

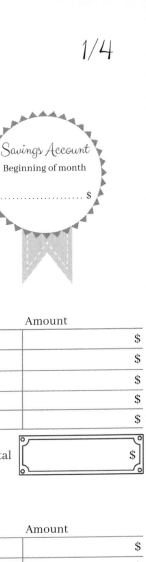

Savings Account

Beginning of month

.... $

Income

Date	Description	Amount
		$
		$
		$
		$
		$

Total $

Fixed Expenses

Date	Description	Amount
		$
		$
		$
		$
		$
		$
		$
		$
		$
		$
		$
		$

Total $

· ·

· ·

How much i want to save : ⌐ . . . . $ ⌐

Income	Fixes Expenses	Savings Goal
. . . . $	− . . . . $	− . . . . $

=

Money available

. . . . $

Estimated spending money

	Week 1	Week 2	Week 3	Week 4	Week 5
Date					
Estimated spending money					
Expenses					

Notes

· ·

· ·

· ·

My categories

1 ....

2 ....

3 ....

4 ....

Expenses

Date	Category	Description	Amount
			$
			$
			$
			$
			$
			$
			$
			$
			$
			$
			$
			$
			$
			$
			$
			$
			$
			$
			$
			$
			$
			$
			$
			$
			$
			$
			$
			$
			$
			$
			$
			$

Total $

Total expenses

Categories

1 . . . . $

2 . . . . $

3 . . . . $

4 . . . . $

Fixes expenses . . . . $

Total expenses | $

Total income . . . . $

Total expenses . . . . $

Money saved . . . . $

Spending wheel

Improvement action

. . . .

. . . .

. . . .

. . . .

Notes

. . . .

. . . .

. . . .

. . . .

Month :

Family Account

Beginning of month

.... $

Savings Account

Beginning of month

.... $

Income

Date	Description	Amount
		$
		$
		$
		$
		$

Total $

Fixed Expenses

Date	Description	Amount
		$
		$
		$
		$
		$
		$
		$
		$
		$
		$
		$
		$

Total $

. . . .

. . . .

How much i want to save : . . . . $

Income	Fixes Expenses	Savings Goal
. . . . $	. . . . $	. . . . $

=

Money available

$

Estimated spending money

	Week 1	Week 2	Week 3	Week 4	Week 5
Date					
Estimated spending money					
Expenses					

Notes

. . . .

. . . .

. . . .

My categories

1 . . . .

2 . . . .

3 . . . .

4 . . . .

Expenses

Date	Category	Description	Amount
			$
			$
			$
			$
			$
			$
			$
			$
			$
			$
			$
			$
			$
			$
			$
			$
			$
			$
			$
			$
			$
			$
			$
			$
			$
			$
			$
			$
			$
			$
			$
			$
			$

Total $

Total expenses

Spending wheel

Categories

1 . . . . $

2 . . . . $

3 . . . . $

4 . . . . $

Fixes expenses   . . . . $

Total expenses [$]

Total income   . . . . $

Total expenses   . . . . $

Money saved   . . . . $

Improvement action

. . . .

. . . .

. . . .

. . . .

Notes

. . . .

. . . .

. . . .

. . . .

Month :

Family Account

Beginning of month

.... $

Savings Account

Beginning of month

.... $

Income

Date	Description	Amount
		$
		$
		$
		$
		$

Total $

Fixed Expenses

Date	Description	Amount
		$
		$
		$
		$
		$
		$
		$
		$
		$
		$
		$
		$

Total $

....

....

How much i want to save : . . . . $

Income	Fixes Expenses	Savings Goal
. . . . $	. . . . $	. . . . $

=

Money available

. . . . $

Estimated spending money

	Week 1	Week 2	Week 3	Week 4	Week 5
Date					
Estimated spending money					
Expenses					

Notes

....

....

....

My categories

1....................
2....................
3....................
4....................

Expenses

Date	Category	Description	Amount
			$
			$
			$
			$
			$
			$
			$
			$
			$
			$
			$
			$
			$
			$
			$
			$
			$
			$
			$
			$
			$
			$
			$
			$
			$
			$
			$
			$
			$
			$
			$
			$

Total $

Total expenses

Categories

1 . . . . $

2 . . . . $

3 . . . . $

4 . . . . $

Fixes expenses   . . . . $

Total expenses | $ |

Total income   . . . . $

Total expenses   . . . . $

Money saved   . . . . $

Spending wheel

Improvement action

. . . .

. . . .

. . . .

. . . .

Notes

. . . .

. . . .

. . . .

. . . .

Month :

Family Account

Beginning of month

.... $

Savings Account

Beginning of month

.... $

Income

Date	Description	Amount
		$
		$
		$
		$
		$

Total $

Fixed Expenses

Date	Description	Amount
		$
		$
		$
		$
		$
		$
		$
		$
		$
		$
		$
		$

Total $

. . . .

. . . .

How much i want to save :

. . . . $

Income		Fixes Expenses		Savings Goal
. . . . $	—	. . . . $	—	. . . . $

=

Money available

. . . . $

Estimated spending money

	Week 1	Week 2	Week 3	Week 4	Week 5
Date					
Estimated spending money					
Expenses					

Notes

. . . .

. . . .

. . . .

My categories

1 . . . .
2 . . . .
3 . . . .
4 . . . .

Expenses

Date	Category	Description	Amount
			$
			$
			$
			$
			$
			$
			$
			$
			$
			$
			$
			$
			$
			$
			$
			$
			$
			$
			$
			$
			$
			$
			$
			$
			$
			$
			$
			$
			$
			$
			$
			$
			$

Total $

Total expenses

Categories

1 . . . . $

2 . . . . $

3 . . . . $

4 . . . . $

Fixes expenses   . . . . $

Total expenses   [$]

Total income   . . . . $

Total expenses   . . . . $

Money saved   . . . . $

Spending wheel

Improvement action

. . . .

. . . .

. . . .

. . . .

Notes

. . . .

. . . .

. . . .

. . . .

Month :

Family Account

Beginning of month

.... $

Savings Account
Beginning of month

.... $

Income

Date	Description	Amount
		$
		$
		$
		$
		$

Total $

Fixed Expenses

Date	Description	Amount
		$
		$
		$
		$
		$
		$
		$
		$
		$
		$
		$
		$

Total $

. . . .

. . . .

How much i want to save : . . . . $

Income	Fixes Expenses	Savings Goal
. . . . $	— . . . . $	— . . . . $

=

Money available

$

Estimated spending money

	Week 1	Week 2	Week 3	Week 4	Week 5
Date					
Estimated spending money					
Expenses					

Notes

. . . .

. . . .

. . . .

My categories

1.................
2.................
3.................
4.................

Date	Category	Description	Amount
			$
			$
			$
			$
			$
			$
			$
			$
			$
			$
			$
			$
			$
			$
			$
			$
			$
			$
			$
			$
			$
			$
			$
			$
			$
			$
			$
			$
			$
			$
			$
			$

 Total $

Total expenses

Categories

1 . . . . $

2 . . . . $

3 . . . . $

4 . . . . $

Fixes expenses   . . . . $

Total expenses   [$]

Total income   . . . . $

Total expenses   . . . . $

Money saved   . . . . $

Spending wheel

Improvement action

. . . .

. . . .

. . . .

. . . .

Notes

. . . .

. . . .

. . . .

. . . .

Month :

Family Account

Beginning of month

.... $

Savings Account

Beginning of month

.... $

Income

Date	Description	Amount
		$
		$
		$
		$
		$

Total $

Fixed Expenses

Date	Description	Amount
		$
		$
		$
		$
		$
		$
		$
		$
		$
		$
		$
		$

Total $

How much i want to save : .... $

Income		Fixes Expenses		Savings Goal
.... $	−	.... $	−	.... $

=

Money available

$

Estimated spending money

	Week 1	Week 2	Week 3	Week 4	Week 5
Date					
Estimated spending money					
Expenses					

Notes

. . . .

. . . .

. . . .

My categories

1....................

2....................

3....................

4....................

Expenses

Date	Category	Description	Amount
			$
			$
			$
			$
			$
			$
			$
			$
			$
			$
			$
			$
			$
			$
			$
			$
			$
			$
			$
			$
			$
			$
			$
			$
			$
			$
			$
			$
			$
			$
			$
			$

Total $

Total expenses

Categories   1 . . . . $

              2 . . . . $

              3 . . . . $

              4 . . . . $

Fixes expenses   . . . . $

Total expenses   [$]

Total income   . . . . $

Total expenses   . . . . $

Money saved   . . . . $

Spending wheel

Improvement action

. . . .

. . . .

. . . .

. . . .

Notes

. . . .

. . . .

. . . .

. . . .

Month :

Family Account

Beginning of month

.... $

Savings Account

Beginning of month

.... $

Income

Date	Description	Amount
		$
		$
		$
		$
		$

Total $

Fixed Expenses

Date	Description	Amount
		$
		$
		$
		$
		$
		$
		$
		$
		$
		$
		$
		$

Total $

. . . .

. . . .

How much i want to save : . . . . $

Income	Fixes Expenses	Savings Goal
. . . . $	. . . . $	. . . . $

=

Money available

. . . . $

Estimated spending money

	Week 1	Week 2	Week 3	Week 4	Week 5
Date					
Estimated spending money					
Expenses					

Notes

. . . .

. . . .

. . . .

My categories
1...................
2...................
3...................
4...................

Expenses

Date	Category	Description	Amount
			$
			$
			$
			$
			$
			$
			$
			$
			$
			$
			$
			$
			$
			$
			$
			$
			$
			$
			$
			$
			$
			$
			$
			$
			$
			$
			$
			$
			$
			$
			$
			$

Total $

Total expenses

Categories

1 . . . . $

2 . . . . $

3 . . . . $

4 . . . . $

Fixes expenses . . . . $

Total expenses | $ |

Total income . . . . $

Total expenses . . . . $

Money saved . . . . $

Spending wheel

Improvement action

. . . .

. . . .

. . . .

. . . .

Notes

. . . .

. . . .

. . . .

. . . .

Family Account

Beginning of month

.... $

Savings Account

Beginning of month

.... $

Income

Date	Description	Amount
		$
		$
		$
		$
		$

Total $

Fixed Expenses

Date	Description	Amount
		$
		$
		$
		$
		$
		$
		$
		$
		$
		$
		$
		$

Total $

....

....

How much i want to save : . . . . $

Income		Fixes Expenses		Savings Goal
. . . . $	**—**	. . . . $	**—**	. . . . $

=

Money available

. . . . $

Estimated spending money

	Week 1	Week 2	Week 3	Week 4	Week 5
Date					
Estimated spending money					
Expenses					

Notes

....

....

....

My categories

1 ....
2 ....
3 ....
4 ....

Expenses

Date	Category	Description	Amount
			$
			$
			$
			$
			$
			$
			$
			$
			$
			$
			$
			$
			$
			$
			$
			$
			$
			$
			$
			$
			$
			$
			$
			$
			$
			$
			$
			$
			$
			$
			$
			$

Total $

Total expenses

Categories

1 . . . . $

2 . . . . $

3 . . . . $

4 . . . . $

Fixes expenses . . . . $

Total expenses | $

Total income . . . . $

Total expenses . . . . $

Money saved . . . . $

Spending wheel

Improvement action

. . . .

. . . .

. . . .

. . . .

Notes

. . . .

. . . .

. . . .

. . . .

Made in the USA
Middletown, DE
20 September 2021